CITY
SLICKER
SPLENDID

Shine Runner Press
shinerunnerpress.com
Blue Springs, MO

copyright: KW Peery
date: 8-8-2025

ISBN: 978-1-7331577-3-5
book design: Hagstone Books

cover image: creative commons

CITY SLICKER SPLENDID

by kw peery

table of contents

TWELFTH & VINE	7
NO SHOT	8
THE UNIVERSE SMIRKS	10
GOOD VIBRATIONS	14
SHOTGUN SPECKLED	15
THIS MOMENT	16
BLEED OUT	17
RUBY	18
PAIR OF TWOS	19
SUSAN	20
REESE	21
BETTYE	22
SHABOOZEY	23
WET A LINE	24
BAD NEWS	25
NEXT TRY	26
ECCENTRIC ESSENCE	27
COUNTRY DUMB	28
CONVINCED	29
PROBLEM WITH PREACHERS	30
SPIRITUAL THANKSGIVING	31
TEN-TEN ON THE SIDE	32
BE NOT AFRAID	33
FREAK FLAG	35

VERBAL MASTURBATION	36
TOO LATE TO BLUFF	37
PURPLE ETHER	38
HANGOVER & HEARTACHE	43
ODESSA	48
WHAT THEY SAY	52
SPIDERWEBBED	55
9:30AM CENTRAL	56
SOUL SHIFTER	57
SEVENTEEN	58
DIVINE	59
MY HAPPY PLACE	61
HEAVY LIFTER	65
SLOW GROWIN' KIND	68
FORTY THREE	72
TANTRIC	73
PHAT BETTY IN DROP D	74
FIVE IN THE FLOW	75
OLD SOFT SHOE	76
APPLESEED	77
PLAY & PRAY	78
NO MAYDAY	79
GOOD ONES	83
TROUBLE WITH THE TRUTH	91
WHERE MY STONED MEETS SOBER	95

TWELFTH & VINE

The kind
Of love
I feel
For you

Hints of
Coleman
Hawkins
And
Charlie
'Bird'

Doin'
GOD'S
Work…

In some
Blue neon
Soaked
After hours
Joint
Off
Twelfth
& Vine

NO SHOT

I'm
As smooth
As the rhythm
Of rain
On This
Roached
Tin roof

Slow sipppin'
On somethin'
80 proof

With the
Scent of
Her shadow
Haunting my
Weary ass
Mind

While
Listenin'
To Leela
Deliver
'Right On Time'

Knowin'
I had
A shot
To save it
Last Summer

But
Was

Too damn
Beat down
Back then
To take it

THE UNIVERSE SMIRKS

If there were
A Richter scale
For fear…
Guilt & shame
Who would we blame

In this
Pseudo-intellectual
Game of
Perceived power
& imaginary control

Those same old
Forlorn faces…
With no
Edge left
To bluff
The battered…
Beaten &
Broken down

Struttin'
Around
With their
Fake ass
Frowns…
Wearin'
Wal-Mart
Crowns
& spineless
Skin suits

Still
Believin'

Their somehow
Bulletproof

Cloaked in
Manufactured
Religion
& concocted
Christianity

Convinced
Of the need
To own
Even more
To Feed

Their
Goddamn greed

While
Sellin' snake oil
As a
Quick cure
For what
Ails us

As
The homeless…
Hungry & hurting
Suffer more…
In forgotten
Neighborhoods

While an
Elected army
Of bribed
Attorneys
Argue over
Scraps
Of a

Sodomized
System
Only serving
The soulless

Those
Fixated on
Feeding an
Imaginary
Scoreboard

Built on
The arthritic
Backs…
Of a poor
Working class

Simple minded
Apostles…
Of a
Self-appointed
King

Sent
To orchestrate
The emptiest
Of all things

For
The sole sake
Of the
Spiritually
Bankrupt

Meanwhile –
The Universe
Smirks

Holdin'

The only
Authentic
Mojo hand...

That
Guarantees
The greediest
Will get
Dealt
The ugliest
Of all
Exits
In the
End

GOOD VIBRATIONS

Brian Wilson
Knows

A good
Vibration
Is the
Lonesome
Voice
Of the
Victor

As she
Rides
Rogue waves
Across the
Dungeons
Down in
Cape Town

SHOTGUN SPECKLED

She was
Milk white
N' freckled

Simply
Shotgun
Speckled…

With an
After hours
Way past
Closin' time
Ms. Piggy tattoo

Located
On the
Outskirts
Of a
Well
Groomed
Runway

Where
I liked
To emergency
Land

When
Nobody else
Would
Save my
Drunk
Cursive
Carcass
At 3AM

THIS MOMENT

To me
The only
Thing
That's ever
Really mattered
Is THIS moment

So
Let's paint
Our
Self-portraits
While listening
To Miles
Make magic
As the
Pharaohs dance

BLEED OUT

Always look
For the light
In darkness

And
Lean
As much
As your
Soul needs
To bleed out
The poison

RUBY

Tranquility
Tames terror
At the source
& reflects back
In deep ruby
Resonance

As
Big Mama
Thornton
Throttles
The Delta
Blues

PAIR OF TWOS

When
Face to face

Fear fails
To distinguish
The difference
Between a
Full house
Or
Richard
Nixon

SUSAN

Witness –
Sarandon in
Silver sequin
On a
Saturday
Afternoon
In June

And she'll
Show you
How the
Sky
Can cause
A tear
From the eye
Any ole time
She chooses

REESE

Witness –
Witherspoon in
Navajo white
And she'll
Turn your lights

Faster than
Any southpaw
Inside the
Squared circle
At
Caesars
Palace

BETTYE

Hearing the
Soulful voice
Of Bettye
LaVette
Is akin to
Witnessin'
A riverside red
Corvette

Slithering
Slow…
Somewhere
Along
Cardinal Circle
Drive
Up in
Muskegon

SHABOOZEY

They say
Slow is smooth
And smooth
Is fast

Kinda like
Watchin'
Shaboozey
Perform
For the
First time
On
Saturday Night
LIVE

Armored in
Viking turquoise
And Elvis
Black leather

WET A LINE

I went out to
Wet a line
And
Caught
Nine

With the
Divine
Echoes
Of Emmylou …

Perched
On the
Fractured
Front steps
Of
Elite Hotel

BAD NEWS

On days
Of rain
I'm reminded
Of her

A fiery
Little redhead
With hair trigger
Temper

The
Somewhat
Exotic brand
Of shadowy
'Bad News'
Luther Allison
Warned me
About

Almost
A
Year
Before
I
Was
Born

NEXT TRY
(For Larry B.)

Mr. Brown
Gave a
Master class
Again

While I
Sat on the
Throne
This mornin'

He reinforced
The fact that
There's always
Enough time
Inside the
Silver lining
Of a
Bad day

To have
A little snort
Before Noon
While making
Difficult
Business decisions
That you
Cannot take back
Until the
Next try

ECCENTRIC ESSENCE

Organized
Religion…
Brand of faith

The choice
Is yours…
To each
Their own

The healthiest
Decision
Likely lies
Somewhere
On the outskirts
Of your
Physical shell

Near the center
Of the core
Of who
You know
You
Truly
Are

COUNTRY DUMB

I may be
Country dumb
In the
Physical sense
But my soul
Speaks fluently
In every
Language

In at least
A thousand
Realms

CONVINCED

I am
Convinced
With 100%
Certainty
That our
Great Creator
Is….
Non-binary

So put
That
In your
Proverbial
Peace pipe
& smoke it

PROBLEM WITH PREACHERS

The problem
I have
With most
Preacher's portrait

Is the way
They choose
To frame things

Weaponizing
Guilt…Fear
& shame

Without care
Or consideration
For the
Long-game

Feeding
Their own
Hungry
Coffers
In the
Name
Of goodness
Despite
Their greed

SPIRITUAL THANKSGIVING

Do not
Allow fear
To play
Your
Heartstrings

Share openly
With unbridled
Trust in
The Great Creator

Every day
Is the
Perfect time
For a
Spiritual
Thanksgiving

TEN-TEN ON THE SIDE

Take a beat
To slow
Your roll
And listen

Give your
Heart
Time to rest
And reset
To a healthier
Rhythm

Then allow
Your soul
To speak first

That
Is the
Essence
You
Wanna
Share
Anyway

BE NOT AFRAID

Be
Not
Afraid…

EVER…

As
Bill Hicks
Explained

This experience
Is just
A ride

So relax…
Kick back

You know
Life…
Like good
Jazz
Is a soundtrack
For the soul

And
If it
Speaks
To yours
Too

May I
Recommend
'Just You…Just Me'
By The

Unique
Thelonious
Monk
Circa
1956

FREAK FLAG

Our spirit
Is ambidextrous

So let
Your
Freak flag
Fly

And
Celebrate
Both sides
Of the sky
As much
As your
Cloudy
Third eye
Needs to

VERBAL MASTURBATION

Verbal masturbation
Is a plague

And
Makes such
A sloppy mess

In those
High priced
Shoes
You're
Sidestepping
The truth
In

TOO LATE TO BLUFF

Grandpa
Always said
There's no
Proof
High enough
To tame
The twisted
truth ---

And
When women
Start askin'
Open
Ended questions...
It's too damn
Late in
The game
To bluff

PURPLE ETHER

I
Don't know
Why I
Miss you

I
Guess it's
Just the
Way it is

I
Know I
Should be
Grateful

But
Somehow your
Still his

Too
Easy to
Run on
Empty

When
I'm almost
Outta fucks

Yeah…
This
Old man
In the mirror
Ain't
The kind

That gives
Shit up

Up in the
Purple ether
Room 333

I'm needin'
You sweet mama
Are you
Still needin'
Me

Like a
Little black dress
On Friday night
So elegant…
Soft & smooth

Here in the
Purple ether
Single malt
&
Blue suede shoes

Yeah-
Here in the
Purple ether

Single malt
&
Blue suede shoes

I
Don't know
How it happened
Our
Energies move
So strange

Just
Another night
In neon
Too stoned
To feel
Your pain

Some
Call me
A hustler…
Cause I'm
Heavier now
Than most

Up in the
Purple ether
Just swingin'
With Petty's
Ghost

Oh-
Here in the
Purple ether
I'm swingin'
With Petty's
Ghost

Up in the
Purple ether
Room 333

I'm needin'
You sweet mama
Are you
Still needin'
Me

Like a
Little black dress

On Friday night
So elegant…
Soft & smooth

Here in the
Purple ether
Single malt
&
Blue suede shoes

Yeah-
Here in the
Purple ether

Single malt
&
Blue suede shoes

So
Take them
Off slow
Sweet mama
While
Freddie plays
The blues

And I'll
Sit back
And relax
Watchin' those
Champagne
Jimmy Choo's

Up in the
Purple ether
Room 333

I'm needin'
You sweet mama

Are you
Still needin'
Me

Like a
Little black dress
On Friday night
So elegant…
Soft & smooth

Here in the
Purple ether
Single malt
&
Blue suede shoes

Yeah-
Here in the
Purple ether

Single malt
&
Blue suede shoes

HANGOVER & HEARTACHE

I'm
In a room
I really
Don't recognize

Head poundin'
A heartbreak
Song

Way
Too many
For a
Wednesday night

Can't remember
Which turn
When wrong

I feel
Like
'The Killer'
Singin' a
Throckmorton
Song

Cruising
Nashville
In an
Eighty-Eight
Olds

I'm
Just a
Hangover

& a heartache

Cheatin'
The odds
Unready
To fold

I'm
A hangover
&
A heartache

Crusin'
Nashville
In an
Eighty-Eight
Olds

I'm
Just a
Hangover
&
A heartache

Feelin'
Guilty…
Too proud
To fold

I'm
A hangover
&
A heartache

On
My knees
In this
Back row
Pew

I'm
Just a
Hangover
&
A heartache
With her
N' still
Needin' you

I'm
Middle aged
Crazy
In
Three quarter
Time

Patsy Cline
Strollin'
Midnight rain

I'm
Stevie pickin'
An Elmore
Joint

Cause
Only James
Knows this
Kind of
Pain

I'm the
First frost
Come
September

Or an
Old flame
Time won't

Erase

I'm
Whitley's
Reflection
In the mirror

With that
Look
Still on
His face

I'm
A hangover
&
A heartache

Crusin'
Nashville
In an
Eighty-Eight
Olds

I'm
Just a
Hangover
&
A heartache

Feelin'
Guilty…
Too proud
To fold

I'm
A hangover
&
A heartache

On
My knees
In this
Back row
Pew

I'm
Just a
Hangover
&
A heartache
With her
N' still
Needin' you

ODESSA

She's
Warm
Smooth
&
Lightnin'
Quick

Makes
Me roll
My own
As she
Licks
Her lips

A
Left handed
Woman
With
Axe handle
Hips

Backwoods
Born…
& Detroit
Slick

Odessa Clay
Odessa Clay
Lips like
A rose
On
New Years
Day

Lead
Me on
& then
Astray

My
Beautiful
Brown mama
Odessa Clay

Make me
Cry…
A little
'Homesick Blues'

Three miles
South
In my
Sunday shoes

Well worth
The blisters…
& all
These dues

Like a
Clean…clear
Liquor
She's warm
N' smooth

Odessa Creel
Odessa Creel
Lips of fire
Make me
Feel unreal

Soft N' salty
Like a

Tater peel
My
Beautiful
Brown mama
Odessa Creel

Feel
The flames
Race against
The night…

A damn
Good lover
In the
Pale moonlight

Smells
Like a
Peach
She's bruised
And ripe

Make a
Bad man
Blush…
And take
His time

Odessa Clay
Odessa Clay
Lips like
A rose
On
New Years
Day

Lead
Me on
& then

Astray

My
Beautiful
Brown mama
Odessa Clay --

Odessa Creel
Odessa Creel
Lips of fire
Make me
Feel unreal

Soft N' salty
Like a
Tater peel
My
Beautiful
Brown mama
Odessa Creel

WHAT THEY SAY

This
Tattered green
Screen door
Is how
Lonely
I feel
Tonight

But
I know
I'm not
Alone
Cause I
Feel my
Spirit Guides

There's
An old
Painted warrior
& a bluesman
On the porch

As Mary
Sings
High harmony
And I face
My last
Divorce

They say
Letting go
Gets easier
Just before
The break

Of day

When
The Moon
Fades to blue
And the hurt
Gets washed away

Oh…
I'm an
Imperfect man
But…well worth
Bein' saved

And
Letting go
Gets easier

At least
That's
What
They say

This old
Square box
Chevy…
She knows
The way back
Home

North of
Sawmill curve
Where the hurt
Stays alone

I can
Feel my
Guardian
Angels…

They protect me
All the time

Even when
I'm a bastard…
Cause
They're the
Forgivin' kind

They say
Letting go
Gets easier
Just before
The break
Of day

When
The Moon
Fades to blue
And the hurt
Gets washed away

Oh…
I'm an
Imperfect man

But…well worth
Bein' saved

And
Letting go
Gets easier

At least
That's
What
They say

SPIDERWEBBED

Two
Spiderwebbed
Silhouettes
Slow tango
With the
Moon

As
Guardian Angels
Giggle
From above
The
Living room

He aches
To taste
The warm
Red wine
Clinging
To her
Lips

As his
Left hand
Traces
Her knowing
Curves

The
Soul
Cannot
Resist

9:30AM CENTRAL

The news of
Uncle Richard's
Passing
Came in
From my
Cousin Bill

I was listening
To Sam Cooke…

Which seemed appropriate

Thanks again…
Uncle Dick

For that
Fat stack
Of 45's…
To feed
My little
Blue
Record player

And all
The memories…
Too many to
Count

You
Know
Which
Ones

SOUL SHIFTER

This mornin'
I reached
The summit
On Kilimanjaro

It took
Seven
Arduous
Days
For my
Soul
To shift

And as
Donald Byrd
Played
'I'm a fool to want you'

An
Angelic choir
Sang soft
In soothing
Refrain

SEVENTEEN

When
The levee
Finally
Gave way

It was
Palm Sunday…

The birds
Sang
Ever so
Softly

And
The only
Thing
My soul
Needed…

Was
To
Wake
Up
Next
To
You

DIVINE

The
Blessings
Roll in
Like thunder
As
Midnight
Finds me
Alone

I
See our
Shadows
Entangled
In tango
And it
Feels
Like
I'm already
Home

It
Reminds me
Of a
Safe place
I'm absolutely
Sure of

There's
Turquoise
Reflections
On our
Silver smiles

An

Incredible
Amalgamation

Only
The
Fearless
Can
Comprehend

MY HAPPY PLACE

This love
Came unexpected
Like a wild
Springtime
Storm

China
Blue eyes
Of wonder
Refusing
To be
Ignored

Wanting you
To want me
To kiss
You

Before
This
Cool rain
Sets on
In

You make
My rhythm
Sweeter

We
Cannot be…
Just
Friends

Truth is

I wasn't
Lookin'
Been fickle
Most my
Life

But
Somethin'
Says I'm
In trouble
It's
Gilded
In the
Stars
This time

Tryin' to
Play it cool
Baby…
Dark shades
And a
Poker face

All
I see
Are diamonds

You…
Are my
Happy place

Yeah –
All
I see
Are diamonds

You….
Are my
Happy place

All
I know
Is the
Moon
Shines
Brighter

When
I wake up
Next
To you

Livin' life
In lavender
And leather
With a hint
Of pink lace
Too

This love
Feels a little
Predestined
I thank
My maker
Every day

The Guardians
Of this galaxy
Know better
Or maybe
Don't
Have the
Stones
To say

Sweet mama
You make my
Feels do
The Watusi

Like
Big Muddy
When she
Ran in
Reverse

It's
Unbelievable
Until we
Let it
Who's
To say
How it
Really works

Tryin' to
Play it cool
Baby…
Dark shades
And a
Poker face

All
I see
Are diamonds

You…
Are my
Happy place

Yeah –
All
I see
Are diamonds

You….
Are my
Happy place

HEAVY LIFTER

Hey there
Heavy Lifter
I can see
Your flow
From here

Keep me
Wondering
If you wanna
Til my
Want to
Disappears

Hey there
Heavy Lifter
Birds signin'
It's almost
Spring

We can
Dance
In the Sun
This
Summer
Baby…
We can do
A lotta things

Yeah…
We'll do
A lotta things

My
Heavy liftin'

Baaaaby
Why are you so blue
Your China eyes
Are bluffin'
Only I can see
The truth

So
Tease me
All ya wanna
My patience
Always pays

My
Heavy liftin'
Baaaaby
These are
Our good ole days

Yeah –
These are
Our good ole days

Hey there
Heavy Lifter
Ya sent a
New Years
Wish
For me

Keep me
Waitin'
If ya wanna
I'll stay busy
With other
Things

Hey there
Heavy Lifter

Good trouble…
Is sometimes
Fun

Especially
When we're
Together
Under the
Makers
Settin' Sun

Oh-
The Makers
Settin' Sun

My
Heavy liftin'
Baaaaby
Why are you so blue
Your China eyes
Are bluffin'
Only I can see
The truth

So
Tease me
All ya wanna
My patience
Always pays

My
Heavy liftin'
Baaaaby
These are
Our good ole days

Yeah –
These are
Our good ole days

SLOW GROWIN' KIND

Turquoise
Skinned knuckles
Still clingin'
To my past

Slow sippin'
Three more
Fingers…
Lonely listnin'
To Johnny Cash

Oh…
Today I
Traded paint
With a shadow
Of myself

While
Guy Clark
Smirked
A little
Knowin'
The truth
Cannot be
Helped

I'm
A rhyme
Wrapped
In riddle
And kin
To the
Hillbilly vine

An oak tree
Amongst the
Timber…
Ya know
The slow growin'
Kind

Yeah…
An oak tree
In the
Timber
The slow growin'
Kind

As the
Angels
Whispered
Softly
I let go
Of shame

Then
GOD
Forgave it
All
And
Evil erased
My name

Now
I'm thunder
Cloaked
Crushed velvet
With a
Rhinestone
James Brown
Cape

Most of

What's been
Said of me
And a hint
Of what
I ain't

I'm
A rhyme
Wrapped
In riddle
And kin
To the
Hillbilly vine

An oak tree
Amongst the
Timber…
Ya know
The slow growin'
Kind

Yeah…
An oak tree
In the
Timber
The slow growin' kind
EIGHT

Since
Most men
Die from
The neck up
At age
Twenty-Five

Why
Does
It take
Eight

Long years
For their
Hearts
To cease
Beating

FORTY THREE
(For Richard B.)

I concede –

It's quite
A feat
For any
Miracle maker
To load
Mercury
With a pitchfork

Or avoid
Cryin' like
A newborn
While reading
Page forty three

TANTRIC
(For Warren Z.)

Eight
Thirty five
Tulsa time

Sipping on
Some
Single origin
Parisi

Listening to
'Reconsider Me'

Patiently
Waiting to see
If the next
Tantric release
Will save me

PHAT BETTY
IN DROP D

When
I asked
Trixie
Why they
Named
The band
'PHAT BETTY DRAPER'

She smirked
And said
Roger Sterling
Pays in
Fat stacks
And wouldn't
Take no
For an
Answer

FIVE IN THE FLOW
(For Hank M.)

Caught
Five in the flow
This mornin'

With a
Wahoo lure

While
Hank Mobley
Played the
'Hipsippy Blues'

OLD SOFT SHOE
(For Kenny D.)

It's a
Damn shame
Kenny's kidneys
Gave out
At forty-eight

'Alone Together'
Still makes my
Ancient soul
Wanna do
The Old
Soft Shoe

APPLESEED

Johnny
Didn't spend
Too much time
Worrying

He knew
Damn well
The seeds
Would bear
Fruit

As soon
As the
Great Creator
Wanted
Them to

PLAY & PRAY
(For Brandon C.)

One time
I heard
Coleman
Say…

Just
Play
&
Pray

Even
If
It
Takes
Another
Decade

What
Else
Do
We
Have
To
Do

NO MAYDAY

They say
Sailors
Love to
Gamble
With GOD
Against
The sea

They know
The storm
Is Comin'
And
He
Helps them…
Believe

It takes
Brains…
Heart & patience
It takes
Guts…
Forged of
Steel

You can
Read it
In their
Knowin' eyes
No bluff…
No choice
No deals

There's
No need

For mayday
When you
Hold the hand
Of faith

It's
Rudder…
Prayer
& courage
Face to face
With fate

They say
It takes
Steady nerve…
On the verge
Of real
Heartbreak

And there's
No need
For mayday
When ya
Hold the hand
Of faith

They say
Sailors
Can feel
Bad weather
Deep inside
Their
Salty bones

Days before
All hell
Breaks loose
When the devil
Won't leav'em

Alone

It takes
Soul…
Strength & trust
Pure belief
Born of grit

You
Can see it
In their
Swagger
When GOD
Won't let'em
Quit

There's
No need
For mayday
When you
Hold the hand
Of faith

It's
Rudder…
Prayer
& courage
Face to face
With fate

They say
It takes
Steady nerve…
On the verge
Of real
Heartbreak

And there's
No need

For mayday
When ya
Hold the hand
Of faith

GOOD ONES

I
Dusted off
Your Bible
And said
Our prayer
Again

Then
Planned to go
Fishin'
But couldn't
Find a
Friend

It's
Not the same
Without ya…
Can't cast
The way
You could

From
That flat
Bottom Jon…
Paris Quarry
When times
Were good

The
Good Ones
Are here
For a
Short time

Like
Whitley
Williams
& Vaughan

Galvanized
In grace
Guardian Angels
And
Patsy songs

There's
A garden
I can
Smell it
Ripe melon
& rich
Black dirt

The
Good Ones
Are here
For a
Short time

And
That's
Just the way
It works

Oh-
The
Good Ones
Are here
For a
Short time

And
That's

Just the way
It works

I've
Loved them
N' left'em
For thrity-four
Lonely years

Been
Heartsick
N' runnin'
From GOD
Shame
And fear

You
Always called me
A winner…
And I believed
It all
Back then

While you
Sang
Pancho & LeftyI sat
Shotgun…
In your
BIG 10

The
Good Ones
Are here
For a
Short time

Like
Whitley
Williams

& Vaughan

Galvanized
In grace
Guardian Angels
And
Patsy songs

There's
A garden
I can
Smell it
Ripe melon
& rich
Black dirt

The
Good Ones
Are here
For a
Short time

And
That's
Just the way
It works

Oh-
The
Good Ones
Are here
For a
Short time

And
That's
Just the way
It works
I'LL DO BETTER

I woke up
Feeling restless
Like there
Was somethin'
Left undone…

So I
Hit rewind
In my
Lovesick mind
But couldn't
Find
The one

The
One place
I always
Lean on…
Where
Most nights
Fade to black

Like steam
On the
Rearview mirror
Or
Last sip
From the
Sack

Yeah-
Steam
On the
Rearview mirror
Or a
Last sip
From the
Sack

Tomorrow
I'll do better
And let the
Worries
Wash away

Turn hard
Right
On my
Way home

Down Old
Number Eight

Maybe…
I'll go
Fishin

And take
More time
To pray….
Yeah –
Tomorrow
I'll do better

Than
I did
Yesterday

Yeah
Tomorrow
I'll do better

Than
I did
Yesterday

I woke up
Feelin' helpless

Like there
Was somethin'
Left undone…

So I
Hit rewind
In my
Lovesick mind
And couldn't
Find
The one

The
One book
I always
Lean on…
Words printed
In bright red
Chapters…
Verses
& numbers

Blood…
Body
Wine
& bread

Yeah –
Chapters…
Versus
& numbers
Blood…
Body
Wine
& bread

Tomorrow
I'll do better
And let the

Worries
Wash away

Turn hard
Right
On my
Way home

Down Old
Number Eight

Maybe…
I'll go
Fishin

And take
More time
To pray….
Yeah –
Tomorrow
I'll do better

Than
I did
Yesterday

Yeah
Tomorrow
I'll do better

Than
I did
Yesterday

TROUBLE WITH THE TRUTH

Alone on
Saturday night
High…
& feelin' low

Blood
Red paint
On canvas
Spirits
Dancin' slow

My heart
He's
Hangin' heavy…
Johnny black
To kill
The blues

Wishin'
I had
Her back…
I'm havin'
Trouble
With the
Truth

I'm havin'
Trouble
With the
Truth

Raised
To be better
Than this

Prayin' for
Better answers
Begging for
One last
Kiss

I've taken
Too many
Chances

My vessel
She's almost
Dry

I'm havin'
Trouble
With the
Truth

And
There ain't
No reason
Why

Oh-
Trouble
With the
Truth

And there
Ain't
No reason
Why

Turntable
Spinnin' Milsap
A one hitter
To ease
The pain

Searchin'
For a
Cleaner
Angle...
To leave
The way
I came

They say
Sin
She'll up
N' gut ya
Then leave
You where
Ya lay

But the
Truth might
Kill me
Quicker...
So who
Am I
To say

I'm havin'
Trouble
With the
Truth

Raised
To be better
Than this

Prayin' for
Better answers
Begging for
One last
Kiss

I've taken
Too many
Chances

My vessel
She's almost
Dry

I'm havin'
Trouble
With the
Truth

And
There ain't
No reason
Why

Oh-
Trouble
With the
Truth

And there
Ain't
No reason
Why

WHERE MY STONED MEETS SOBER

It's
Nine forty five
And the
Hybrids
Kickin' in

Ridin'
Rogue waves
With a
Quicksilver
Grin

I've got
The Ozark Blues
On shuffle
And magic
In this tea

Wearin'
Kingman
Turquoise
And Prada
With an
Ace up
My sleeve

Where my
Stoned meets sober
The brutal truth
Unwinds

I wanna

Tell you baaaby…
But
I don't
Have the time

I'm a
Lonely soul
Searchin'…
In three quarter
Time

Where my
Stoned meets sober
The brutal truth
Unwinds

Yeah –
Where my
Stoned meets sober
The brutal truth
Unwinds

Muddy used
To tell me…
This World
Can be
Cruel

And when
Gibbons
Hits a lick
It's pure
Damn
Rocket fuel

So I
Dose
When I
Need to

Cause high vibe
Is the game

Don't mind
The details
No need
To fan
These flames

Where my
Stoned meets sober
The brutal truth
Unwinds

I wanna
Tell you baaaby…
But
I don't
Have the time

I'm a
Lonely soul
Searchin'…
In three quarter
Time

Where my
Stoned meets sober
The brutal truth
Unwinds

Yeah –
Where my
Stoned meets sober
The brutal truth
Unwinds

Americana songwriter and Kansas-City-based storyteller K.W. Peery is the author of sixteen poetry collections. He is founder and editor of The Angel's Share Literary Magazine (Shine Runner Press).

His work is included in the Vincent Van Gogh Anthology Resurrection of a Sunflower, The Cosmic Lost and Found: An Anthology of Missouri Poets (Spartan Press), The Konza Poetry Project Presents: Somewhere Between Kansas City And Denver (Spartan Press) and Best of Mad Swirl Anthology. Peery's work has been published in The Main Street Rag, Chiron Review, San Pedro River Review, The Gasconade Review, Big Hammer, Blink Ink, Rusty Truck, Mad Swirl, Veterans Voices Magazine, Mojave River Review, The Asylum Floor, From Whispers to Roars, Fearless Poetry Zine, Culture Cult Magazine, Punk Noir, Mutata Re and The Beatnik Cowboy.

Credited as a lyricist and producer, Peery's work appears on more than twenty studio albums over the past decade.

www.ingramcontent.com/pod-product-compliance
Lightning Source LLC
Chambersburg PA
CBHW050225100526
44585CB00017BA/2050